NOW FAITH

Planting a Seed of Faith: #1

Wanda Cheeks

NOW Faith: Planting a Seed of Faith: #1
Published by INSPIRED2INSPIRE, LLC.
© 2021 Wanda Cheeks. All rights reserved.

No part of this book may be reproduced, distributed, or transmitted in any form, by any means, graphics, electronics, or mechanical (including photocopy, recording, taping, or by any information storage or retrieval system), without written permission from the publisher, except in the case of reprints in the context of reviews, quotes, or references.

Printed in the United States of America
ISBN: 978-1-7369154-2-4

Dedication

God, I thank you for every storm, drought, trial, test, and battle. It just shows the truth of how you are always with me. I am nothing without you. So here I am, a willing vessel ready to serve as you need. Have your way and get the complete glory from my life.

For bookings, send your requests to admin@inspired2inspire.co using the subject line BOOKINGS. For more information (or if you're a book club, association, organization, or special interest group interested in bulk orders, contact admin@inspired2inspire.co using the subject line BULK ORDER).

TABLE OF CONTENTS

Introduction 1

Chapter 1: Seed 5

Chapter 2: Roots 13

Chapter 3: Seasoned 21

Chapter 4: Green House 31

Chapter 5: EverGreen 43

Chapter 6: In the House 51

Chapter 7: Harvest 57

's Journal 67

INTRODUCTION

This is for you! If you are alive and breathing right now, this is for you! If you are going through anything in your life at all, this is for you. If you deal with anxiety, fear, hurt, emotional damage, attachment issues, or anything else in this ballpark, this is for you. If you are looking to start a project, a book, a degree and finish it, this is for you. If you are looking to start a business or work your way towards retirement, this is for you. If you have a lack anywhere in your life, whether it be time, resources, answers, a way out, and the most common MONEY, this is for you! If you feel like life is what it is and you have to settle, this is for you. If you are looking simply for a miracle, this is for you! If you are a believer of Christ or not, this is for you!

Throughout this book, you will journey with me in the current stages of my faith walk leading to my next. In walking with me, you will be guided and equipped with questions to understand where you are in yours. The intention is to understand what faith would look like concerning your need or desire and ultimately give you the option to plant the seed of faith. You will be given some biblical truths in comparison to what it looks like for me and what it could look like for you. Be open-minded!

While I am the one asking these questions, I want to make a quick disclaimer and let you know I am really not that deep. I'm not one who is high holy or who has it all figured out, but who I am is someone that has reaped the benefits of faith and has watched my life change tremendously.

Just like most others, I am still figuring out this faith walk but I am willing to go on the journey. I am not yet a billionaire or living in a fancy house with a fancy car, but I stand secure on what and who I believe in. I am resting on the foundation of every mountain that I have been brought over leading me to this point of writing a book. As this is my encounter with following God coming from a place where I had lost faith in everything and everyone, I believe in my heart that this is an opportunity for believers and non-believers to reap the harvest of what great faith looks like.

I don't take this opportunity lightly as this is not a moment of persuasion but a moment of understanding the power of possibilities. This is to gain or restore hope for those things we've lost hope for.

In writing this, my goal is not to gain a group of people who may only consider taking a leap of faith but to actually do it. As my faith is being tested, I'm learning about the surface-level issues we have on a daily basis that don't get addressed. This doesn't even account for all the deeper moments in the process that we may encounter that no one sees.

As I share my experience, I hope that you are encouraged to leap, jump, hop, skip and walk this road, plant a seed, accomplish something that hasn't been or what needs to be accomplished again.

We all have to start somewhere. So I am starting with this book!

This has been undoubtedly the most challenging experience I have ever encountered in all of my 25 years of living; Writing a book, telling my business and actually doing the work to overcome the hardest trial I have been facing. As much as I fought about not wanting to do any of it at all I knew in my heart it is bigger than me.

I've always had the vision but no execution. In my complacency, laziness, overthinking, and my self-doubt, I struggled for years on writing a book in general. This particular book Months of my head being flooded with the words to say but no idea how to get it on paper. My improper grammar, current situation surrounded by a lifestyle of poverty, and my little faith had consumed me. I dwelled in every excuse around me. My bank account argued that I couldn't publish a book, and my job supported its statement. I had little influence, I thought if the book would even sell. The chaos around me started getting a little cozy and I learned to function in it. Never feeling like I had the time or the resources to complete it was the biggest lie I told myself because somehow I had the time and resources for everyone and thing else.

In November of 2022, God pushed me to try faith. In hearing God tell me to trust him I bought a ticket to Healher 2023 conference. I didn't know any but one speaker on the program. I had no clue how I was going to secure my bills, get there, and where I was going to stay. With everything going on, going to a conference was the last thing on my mind. But I just kept hearing God say trust me; So, I did!

In prayer, I said, "God if I'm going to this conference I need to get the time off." At this moment my job was taking no more requests for time off and I got the time off no problem. I then said, "God, you've given me the time off but (as I laughed) I need you to drop that price cos I ain't got it right now." When I tell you I looked down at my watch and saw a notification for the conference saying "just for today" and the price had dropped. I instantly bought a ticket. I did panic a little right after (my faith was still a little weak. Don't judge me).

A couple of days later I said, "Well God, I have got the time off and a ticket but no money or means for staying. You've carried me this far. What else do you have for me?" Not only did God provide the way for me to go and a place to stay, he even took care of the bills that I was worried about. I drove what was supposed to be nine hours by myself (it took twelve). God protected me and provided for me every step of the way. I was blessed and my life had been changed forever. I couldn't have only heard the word, but this time when I went back home there was a charge to work the word I was given and so I did.

This was the leading point for me to even think I could write a book and conquer the giant that I'm facing.

As I have said before I was looking at something bigger than me, and that was exactly why it had to be conquered. I saw the results of what it was to trust God. Why not trust him again.

Believing that this was given to me by God I had to realize that the bigger picture was that one story can change someone's life, even my own. The biggest picture is that God can get the glory! Yes, even out of someone like me; Somebody basic. I don't have a history of authors or anything like it in my family. It feels good to be the first! In this process I'm learning that God just wants my trust, obedience, and effort and everything else will fall in line accordingly. So here I am 1:30 am August 20, 2023 at the table typing as if I don't have church in a few hours.

I say all of this to simply tug on your faith. You never know what is waiting for you on the other side of your faith. Faith is fueled on your belief, your ability to get up and go, your ability to do it afraid and your ability to fail until you succeed. Your mess can easily turn into your message and your test into your testimony with one decision. Your change could be right now. Just have FAITH!!!

CHAPTER 1

SEED

I truly find it amazing that we are really out here surviving the 21st century! I had this ongoing joke that wasn't really a joke, saying "I was born in the wrong time because I am not like these people at all." And I'd usually follow with "This is ghetto." I hear the words "anxiety," "trauma," and "triggered" more than anything. There is so much identity confusion, religious corruption and to top it all off, there is such a "cancel" culture that puts a tight leash on anyone who has an opinion or even a fact that disagrees with another. I'm telling you, "GHETTO!" This generation we are witnessing are such sensitive yet reckless people in an already chaotic world. It doesn't mix. It's even scarier the fact that we are watching the book of revelations play out right before our eyes and many people are so oblivious and or numb to it. There is such a lack of reverence, respect, recovery, rejoicing, reconciliation, revival, repentance, and even reevaluation for the reality in which we live.

I'm not a big history person but I do love to sit and listen to the stories told by those that came before me. I listened to the struggles they had to face. Some of the things I've heard were about their mental battles, dealing with the detriment of their own decisions or decisions from others that just so happened to land on them. I even listened to the things that were out loud that affected their personal lives such as the laws, restrictions and cruelty faced due to them just being. These are many of the same things we are up against today. There is so much war in our minds, within ourselves, within our homes, with people, placement, and literally around the world. We too are left dealing with the decisions we've made and that others made concerning us. A lot of the time we are left with puzzle pieces and no end picture trying to figure it out. What's really hard is that there is so much more influence and things we are exposed to that make protection nearly impossible.

Times really have changed; but as I sit here, I ponder over the fact that even with all the struggles faced by those of yesteryear, there was somewhere in the story where there was a moment of conquering. Somehow we ended up here. How we got here is not in question, the point is the fact that we are here. So then we are left with the question: Why? Why here? Why with these people? Why now? Out of every story I've heard, the ones that really tattooed itself to my heart are their stories of victory. Their stories of overcoming and pushing forward to tell their story. It also helps me to reflect on every moment that came before me that helped me to live in the freedom that I have today. I reflect on how today as a young black female I am able to pursue an education. I can work, go to school, and congregate amongst different genders, races and communities when that wasn't the case beforehand. I'm telling you it was real grace that I never had to work in somebody's field, or necessarily have to be separated from my family because of it.

When I look at the things we have available to us now, I am left in awe. We are living in a time of robots, machines and prototypes for personal flying devices. These were all once just small ideas, dreams, and visions.

Something someone believed for and now we are reaping the harvest of just that. We are reaping the harvest of someone pushing past the sight, reality and difficulties of what was named nonexistent/ impossible. We are reaping the harvest of someone's visions, process and ability to execute. Someone's decision to live a life using what they had to get what they wanted to see. We are simply reaping the harvest of what Faith and works look like. With all of this, I then consider as we are reaping a harvest, there will soon be a need for replanting for both us and the next generation to reap a harvest from. Maybe that is exactly why we are here. What if we are the next to believe in the impossible? What if we are the next to change what could've, should've and would've been for what is coming? Maybe we are planted in this time, place and with these people and things to change them, us, our families, friends, etc. We are the next generation of faith. Honestly we need it. Just turning on the Tv or scrolling through social media we see so much tragedy, death, sickness, poverty, pain, and the list goes on. Many of us reading this have our own personal issues that could use a miracle, hope, help, healing and/or some sort of change. We also have so many people stuck in their ways and many people worried about others and completely unaware of their own issues. These days we need eyes opened. We need prayers answered. We need clear minds. We need a new normal.

Even as I write this today, I can identify places where I myself found comfort in chaos, a "living" in lack, and where I've made myself malleable to a broken mindset. It took others around me acknowledging the concerns of my life as "not normal" for me to even slightly open my eyes to the reality of my displacement. It was easier for someone looking in from the outside to see me more than I could see myself. I didn't understand that there was a need for more because I didn't know that there was a presence of lack. Something that is often failed to do, is one taking the time to evaluate and process the reality of the cards they are dealt. We typically see no change in the "uncommon" as it is so commonly unidentified.

When was the last time you've really looked at your hand? I want you to really reflect on your life right now! Are you okay? What is something you want to see happen in the world? What is something you want to see happen in your own personal life? What goals and desires do you have on your mind? Do you have any illnesses in your body or in your bloodline? Do you wrestle with anxiety, fear, or grief? Are there any concerns with finances, friends, families, or loved ones that were brought to your attention? Can you identify anything? Write these things down and reflect on the impact it has on you. Now start to envision what it would look like if it changed.

These things that we've considered are some of the factors that contribute to our everyday lives. This reflects in our reactions, our responses, and even our current character that we present whether it is public or private information. As you are looking over the things that you may want a miracle for, I'm challenging myself to do the same. I am beyond grateful for how far God has taken me. I'm not even the same person that entered into this current year. Even in my gratefulness there is something within me desperate and crying out for more. At this glorious age of a quarter of a century, I am almost entering into a fourteen year cycle of displacement. Almost fourteen years of moving from place to place, never settling or actually calling a place home. Almost fourteen years of learning routines, covering up and just settling for the fact that I don't entirely look like what I am going through. This was almost fourteen years of never seeing beyond what I am physically seeing. I look at the time span. I look at the depths of my truth. I look at the things that came to be that came from nothing. Now I look at an issue that has potential and I see a reason to believe. I see a reason to have faith.

Faith! A word that has become a common luxury of a phrase that honestly is often misused.

> "Now faith is the substance of things hoped for, the evidence of things not seen."
>
> -Hebrews 11:1 KJV

When we look at the defining word "hope" we can perceive this is toward a joyful anticipation for something that is desired. When we see a listing for a job that we may want, there is a hope within us to rejoice and anticipate getting the job. Where does faith fit in? Faith squeezes itself in where there is an unlikeliness for it to happen but we believe beyond the likeliness and apply for the job anyway. I hear the mix up of faith when it's applied to those things that we have control over. If you are believing that you will not argue with somebody today, believe no further because it takes two to argue. You have control over it. If your hope is in having a full paycheck, just show up to work. You have control over it. If you hope to receive an encouraging message, show up or listen to something encouraging with anticipation and openness to receive and you can have just that. The faith I'm talking about is faith to believe that cancer can be cured, grief can be consumed with fresh joy, babies can be born through infertility. I'm talking about reduced sentences for locked up children, prayer that reaches the classrooms being exemplified or being in the right frame of mind. The faith to be married to who is meant for you, to see a turnaround in finances, relationships, and or self. Faith for those things that need more than just our own capabilities. What I am in right now, I'm telling y'all there is no way I was able to see my way out of it. I couldn't even see myself in it. When I did become aware of this issue I was too embarrassed to ever talk about it. Every attempt I made fell right through my hands. As unstable as my mind was, so was everything else. I was curious but comfortable. I was tired but I guess not tired enough.

> "A double minded man is unstable in all his ways."
>
> -James 1:8 KJV

I needed something to push me beyond myself. I needed to be able to see beyond the lack of finances, connections, and my own convinced mind that there was nothing more for me. A messed up mind can cause a messed up future.

I am one of those kids that grew up in church literally all of my life. I know how to church. I know how to call and respond. I know how to sing hymns and quote cliches and scripture. I know learned behavior. What I didn't know was what having faith in God was about.

I've seen all the accomplishments that I felt I had achieved without the help of "This God". I looked at my circumstances and really thought about "where is he in all of this?". I was so convinced I had this all figured out and look where I still am.

If you are anything like me, there is a possibility that trust issues may be present (the Lord is yet working on me). I, at a time, had no desire or interest in investing my ideas unto someone who was not physically in front of me. If I barely trust the people who I can see, what makes you think I could trust who I can't see? And so even in my expression of faith I also have to consider those who may say "I mean I'm doing pretty okay without necessarily believing in God". Maybe the situation is "I don't really understand all of that". Maybe the issue is "I have put my faith in God", "I've prayed about it", and/or "I've tried Jesus" and feel like something went wrong in the process. Maybe it seems like you can't catch a break, maybe you weren't protected from something that hurt you, maybe you've prayed for someone to get better and God took them home instead, maybe it's multiple losses, maybe even praying a simple prayer and feeling like it hasn't been answered. So why invest faith in him?

If someone were to give you an offer to choose a dollar or a million dollars, what would you choose? Any sane person would have answered for a million dollars. We as natural beings want more! God is simply an offer for more. Someone may ask how. Well again not a history person but we look at history books and man-written documents that record all moments up to this point and we believe it. I realize, many including myself disregarded the bible as a historical documentation also recording past events.

> "So then faith cometh by hearing, and hearing by the word of God."
>
> **- Romans 10:17 KJV**

This same historical documentation flat out tells me that he can handle my impossible.

> "...The things which are impossible with men are possible with God."
>
> **- Luke 18:27 KJV**

When I browse through the bible even slightly, we see creation formed by him speaking. We hear about seas splitting to bring a people out of captivity. We hear of people being cured of lifelong and or long-time ailments. Just as much as I believed in Santa Clause, why not take a chance and believe in someone who has a greater ability than I do to provide. I don't want the resource, I want the source. I don't want the natural, I have that. I need a super to my natural. Honestly even if that wasn't enough what do we really have to lose.

Realistically the whole idea of believing in God is killed by a false image through people misrepresenting his name. It is also killed by unrealistic expectations in this world of free choice. This is where we start asking those questions of "where is this God in my circumstances?" when it is documented that we have free choice. It's not a discussion of his presence but our willingness to allow him to be actively a part of our choices. If we choose to spend rent money on random shopping and wonder why he allows you to be broke becomes an issue of your own choice. Also there is sometimes this idea that things have to be done a certain way or it wasn't right. Like those that prayed and believed for healing and that person passed away. Sometimes we don't change our perspective to see that maybe death was the way of healing. Maybe prison was a form of protection or not having riches was a form of breaking reckless spending habits.

I admit, I did not easily budge myself. It took a moment where I could not provide in any way for myself to try God for real. I was already "Homeless" and now I physically could not work and had car payments, bills, and the need for gas money and food. A month without my own resources and yet I kept my car, gas tank stayed full and not a night I went without food in my belly unless I chose not to eat. I never asked for help (because I was too prideful), yet still had everything I needed. This alone was something bigger than me. As I stay in another place bedless, with a low waged job, and really nothing to offer but my ability to write about faith, I am left to try God for what was bigger than that last moment I faced. I've built a relationship with him, learning him as a keeper in this dark season but now I want to know him as the God who can see me into my exceeding and abundant overflow.

I believe that one day I will be able to fund housing buildings for others experiencing homelessness and possibly even fund someone's idea that they have faith in. More than just what will happen for me, I'm deciding to believe we will one day hear stories in these times of the blind gaining sight, deaf hearing, captives being set free, bodies and minds healed, broken souls made whole and the ability of the next generation to reap the harvest of faith that is within us.

We are all living out lives brought to us by decisions made by somebody. Not everyone is going through a rough season but everyone is facing something. Someone may be left with a decision to make space for something new, unusual, uncomfortable, that brings change, or that keeps them praying. Whatever the decision is, you ultimately have an option right now to decide you are going to believe beyond what you see. Will you consider planting a seed of faith with me?

CHAPTER 2
ROOTS

I must ask the question, are you living on the surface? What I mean by this is, are you living without a deeper understanding of who you are or your "why" right now? Experiencing NY every day, I get to witness some outlandish stuff. This could be me going past someone who is walking in circles, yelling at themselves in the middle of the busiest streets or news reports that the city is sinking literally! As human as I am, it is often that I could walk past a person like that with a side-eye, not considering what got them to that point in the first place. In the same token, I'm usually wishing someone would understand me.

You see, it is very easy to dismiss the crisis around us when we have to consider on a daily basis the crisis, cause, and conscience within us. While we can learn to ignore and not find interest in anyone or thing not directly concerning us, what I find fascinating is realistically we learn to ignore or block out the things concerning ourselves more than anything. As we are in contact more with the consistencies of who we are, I speak for myself acknowledging that I personally didn't take much time connecting dots of my make-up, my DNA, my thinking, and really why I desire the things I desire. If we have survived this long without, what's the need for it now?

When we think about planting a seed, we know that if you plant a seed for a rose, you will get a rose. If you plant oranges, you won't get apples; you will get oranges. These are the obvious factors of planting. Well, these are the very same results that come when we plant our seeds of faith. If I can take a moment to be transparent, before I decided to plant this very seed of faith believing for my next, I planted a seed believing for the same thing but instead of planting in faith I did it in anger and hurt. I had become so hurt by the people I expected to help me or took from me knowing I didn't have much. I let anger fester after grieving stages of rejection. I started to plan my own way out of poverty and it was solely to prove a point. After all of that, I was left with more anger and hurt from my failed plans.

In this new walk for me, I am starting to pay more attention to projects, goals, and anything else I start and seem to struggle to finish. Yes, I used to be the one that would have a New Year resolution and break it by May. I had to take time to really examine my excuses of why I hadn't accomplished what I set out to accomplish. The more and more I tried and failed the more frustrated I'd become to the point of no longer wanting to try. Then taking a second look, I realized my failure to commit and execute in certain areas were deeper than just the surface. I had created gardens off of my brokenness and failed to see with my blurred perspective, so I couldn't see things through. Brokenness, blindness, anger, hurt all came from something deep down.

When thinking about my faith right now I see myself in parallel with the Israelites in the book of Exodus. People who were in a place of bondage and needed to be rescued. As I look back at the Israelites in their time of bondage in Egypt I am grieved by the reality of why they were overtaken in the first place. One thought and decision of another changed many lives and futures. The new Pharaoh of that time didn't like the power the Israelites possessed as they were growing in number and kept increasing. This could potentially mean the Israelites turning against them and overtaking Egypt if this situation wasn't under control. In his decision making, many were oppressed, killed, forced into hard labor, and generations to come would also be born into this broken lifestyle.

Do you recall any portions of your life that you were handed down, born or raised into, pulled or pushed into something that had nothing to do with you originally? Consider things like poverty, drug or alcohol usage. Maybe your parents collided without considering the fact both sides had a little crazy in them, or mental, emotional, and/or physical illnesses connected to them. Maybe generational curses got passed down. Maybe there was a love that was given that is hard to replicate. You can even consider a career, calling, mantle or personality trait. Maybe an idea that has your attention. Lastly, just for ideas to reflect on, consider the reality of your dreams, goals, or desires that hit a brick wall because the money, resources, ability and/or time are not yet in your possession. If any, how have you been affected?

Believe it or not, these things are what commonly drive our intentions and even our hopes in planting a seed at all. If someone is brought up in a loving family, their seed of faith may reflect an attempt to recreate that loving environment. Even if it's the opposite, maybe they'd want to build something they never had. Someone who's been single for a long time or failed relationships may plant a seed believing to find their forever because right now something in them wants to feel that love. There is a root to every cause.

Personally, as I ended up with this seed to plant, I really struggled with how I got it in the first place. My mother was one of the hardest working people I could ever know. It didn't matter how tired, sick or stressed she was; she went to work. My mother could be out of the hospital one day and clocked in the next. She is not only a hard worker but someone with such a gift of a creative mind. But even as persistent as my mother was, she has never been a friend in fellowship with finances. This meant minor shopping prices but not minor shopping. This meant with my mom's heart of gold, feeding the world even if that meant her not eating herself. This meant giving help that one day she wouldn't receive in return in some areas. This meant being rejected. This meant taking a fall that was a little hard to get back up from. Life just happened.

Not too long ago the words were spoken to me "You are just like your mother". As harmless as this statement could be, it has a pretty big sting coming from someone who views her life as a failing one. Understanding that not one word in the statement was false, I realized the impact that those words had on me. I had not only received her creative mind but her heart too. Not only her heart but her habits. Not only her habits but her hurt. What amazes me is that all of it didn't start with her. Going back to my grandmother and her mother and even beyond that rejection was present. Placement in standards of homes were already out of whack. Help was a hated word as it was mishandled. The sad part is no one saw it so no one stopped it and generations later here I am with it in my hands. A torch at times I wish was never passed down. The Israelites too had a torch passed down and they held for four hundred years!

Hard labor, oppression, and cruel treatment had become the fate of something that just happened to the Israelites. Infertility, grief, some sicknesses, death, bills, passed down jobs, and titles are some examples of life just happening and then we are left saying "Okay, now what do we do next?" Let's first stand assure that there is hope alone in the fact that something always comes next.

Next for the Israelites just so happened to be an open door to leave their troubles behind them and walk into the greatness of a land filled with more than they thought they would ever see. They finally caught a glimpse of light but still struggled through the sight of the garden created from their roots. Something needed to be cut.

40 is the number of years they endured the wilderness after being pulled from captivity. Forty years of retaliation, disobedience, and wavering belief. Forty years of repeated cycles after they already walked away from the biggest thing they had faced thus far. And it leaves me with

the question, "why in the world would they willingly question or rebel against the possibility of better?" Why do we struggle to believe?

Looking at their open door to walk into freedom and a promised land we could look at the situation and think how crazy they were for how they responded and what we would've done if it was us. With these same thoughts in mind I personally had to reconsider my position and say maybe their thinking was justified in the beginning.

As much as I'd love to sit back and point the finger and say "this could never be me", My reality is that it is me right now. I can dwell and focus on the beginning of my fourteen years but I also have to shift focus and pull at the root of the last seven years of the fourteen. These last seven years I have reached an age (Maybe not of maturity but an age) where I was able to be removed from this situation. What kept me stuck? Back in Egypt the Israelites were (for lack of better words) programmed. For four hundred years they were conditioned to captivity Manipulated into being minor and were now trying to build faith on broken beliefs. They encountered much loss, fear, and hurt and it reflected in the way they maneuvered. In the same token while all of this was going on they were still provided for. While being in the desert they faced the light of new fear while having to entrust the source of provision into someone they weren't familiar with. As frustrating as it could be to read, this (plus their stubbornness) supported their idea not to fully trust God because of what they experienced and what they were already used to.

Facing infertility and having constant negative results can do this to someone. Inability becomes a root. Stepping into a place of authority with high expectations knowing what came before can do this to someone. Fear of disappointment, disapproval, or mismanagement can become a root. Small moments of joy not matching the pain of loss can do this to someone. Inconsistencies become a root. The roots keep our mindsets in positions that deter us from the faith to believe that something good can come from what we are up against no matter what the options are.

This is how I had become comfortable in what I was conditioned to. I've gone years without an actual bed, complete access to all things of where I resided, and yet I've been making the decision to stay in it. This is what I knew, and fear and uncertainty have kept me from taking a step off sure ground. I allowed fear to dictate my thinking, my hearing, my sight, and the picture of a new vision.

It was easy to see that my mom struggled, so why wouldn't I? I saw constant incompleteness in walking into open doors and followed pursuit. This is why I needed something bigger than me to pull me out. In this particular part, I found myself knowing what it feels like, questioning "where is this God and how does he play a part in my story?"

Now, this is the part where I can really get excited. This God I had found myself questioning did something that was so needed. He saw. As he sees, he sends something to intervene. He saw Israel and intervened; he saw me and intervened, and he sees you and is willing to intervene on your behalf as well.

For the captives of Egypt, he sent Moses. A man who saw himself as incapable, unqualified, and inadequate, but it just so happened he was just the right person for the job. As we look at ourselves, we have to be willing to adapt to the idea that we are enough to see the moment through when we walk with God, killing every root that discourages us. All Moses had to do was make a decision.

Fear, comfort, hurt, "I don't know," and "there's nothing I can do about it" have had control of many of us for far too long! This is our time to take control out of their hands and place it in God's hands. If it was brought to us, something may have needed to be brought through us. This is Faith.

God made no mistake when he allowed me to be born in the midst of all this displacement. He made no mistake allowing me to dwell in it. He made no mistakes bringing it to my attention. He made no mistake giving me the desires of my heart to want more. And he made no mistake making me just like my mother. He made no mistakes with you either!!!

Even with the mind manipulation passed down, I have to take in that I also received my mother's creativity and hard work. Her story told one thing, but there is something about a sequel. This is an opportunity for an author or creator to take a similar thing and change something about it. This could mean small details or even how the story ends. Our cover of the story may look the same, but I guarantee my ending won't. I will complete what I am starting, and I have faith that she will too.

Just like someone else's decisions fell on my family and landed on me, mine will fall on someone else. I am determined that when it hits my children, my story won't be theirs. They will be born into something better than I did. I am making a choice now to trust God, to believe him and take him at his word. His word tells me in Psalms 34:19 NKJV that many are the afflictions of the righteous, but it also says that the Lord will deliver me out. I may have failed in some areas, but I know he won't.

God used a man who had his own roots, past, thoughts, and concerns to carry a large body of people through the process of cutting their roots heading into their greater. What is amazing is that his roots at the time were being cut in the same process. Infertility can cut roots for a child without a home while also cutting the roots of a parent being childless; Or even prove that faith and waiting can change the outcome encouraging and cutting roots of someone else experiencing the same.

A small disappointment to someone can break fear and cut roots of tradition. Grieving and fully taking time to process cuts the roots of being bound to grief. Learning how to create and strive for consistent joy cuts roots. Believing you can start the business cuts the roots. Belief in general can cut roots.

For Israel, it took forty years to get to the promised land, for me, I believe it is soon to come, and for you, it can and will be too. Whatever was placed in your hands, brought to your attention, fell on your heart can and will see the fruit of your seed of decision. No matter what happened before this moment, NOW is an opportunity to believe that there is more for you.

Fear, doubt and lack of resources will not control what will soon fall into your hands. Your belief will. You CAN be healed, whole, and given the finances you need. You CAN be free from whatever it is that you need to be free from. You CAN have whatever you need to have. Root up anything that leads you to believe otherwise. Look at what it is you have and make a decision and plant your seed in good ground so that you may reap a good harvest.

What are some things you are uprooting? How can you change or add insight to your vision of harvest? What do you believe about yourself?

CHAPTER 3
SEASONED

My favorite time of year, due to its significance and beauty, is none other than the best season of all, Autumn. This marks the beginning of the transition from warm weather to sweater weather. In the midst of this transition, as we look outside, we recognize the change in the colors of the leaves. We notice flowers that once were, starting to fall. This becomes a time of harvest for the last of the summer fruits and perfect conditions for homemade pumpkin seeds and candy apples.

In this time of year, gardeners and farmers take time to prepare their land, crops, animals, and selves for the changes that are due to occur. These field workers are knowledgeable, skilled, and equipped with every tool needed to keep their fields ready for what is to come. Not only for what is to come immediately after, but they prepare themselves for what will be at a later point.

Gardeners and farmers not only prepare their fields for each season but they do so making sure what is planted is in position for transition and/or placed for grace to receive everything needed for them to prosper. This could mean the appropriate amount of rain, sunlight, air, shade, and shelter being provided. They are aware that all of it is necessary for not only the growth but the harvest of what they are planting. This is just a process preparing for production.

We took a lot of time talking about uprooting and cutting away at those things we can identify as potential threats to our seeds but didn't really converse concerning the cost of time, work, and self it requires to be accomplished. Everything we encounter in life comes with a process. It can be a healing process or even as simple as waiting for your order to ship and get to you. This is just the reality of things.

A natural seed in the ground usually takes some time before it starts showing face. By this time it has already faced rain, sunshine, storms, day and night and whatever else crossed its path. The beauty of it is that no matter what comes its way, it stays planted. The even more beautiful part is that after undergoing the process of uprooting, it makes room for rerooting fresh under the ground.

When I think about my seed, the cry of my heart, the anticipation in my mind and all of the humanity within me screams for me to have what I want right now. I haven't necessarily asked for a deep revelation of my whole planting situation, but I had to eventually allow it to settle in my mind that the bigger my promise is, the bigger the patience and purpose in the process will be. It is not an overnight event.

Today, sadly, we are amongst a microwave generation. We have the luxury of DoorDash, Uber, and everything we need access to right at our fingertips. In many areas, we don't have to put much effort into it, so patience and work are usually things we don't invest in. This is where we see a lot of people start to doubt.

One major thing about the field workers is not the fact that they are willing to wait and work, but it's the fact that they know what they are waiting and working for. It has value to them. To some, it may not just be a meal but income. For our own seeds no matter how big or small, they have their own measure of value.

Every seed of faith will have to endure its own form of season and weathering.

> "To every thing there is a season, and a time to every purpose under the heaven."
>
> -Ecclesiastes 3:1 KJV

Your willingness to go through the process is determined by its true value to you. This is why we see many people start and not finish what they set out to. For me, I finally got tired of my destructive thinking and aching bones at the age of 25. Like I said, changing my life before was about proving points, but now to me, it is about being an example. Yes, I want to finally get a bed and keys to my own place, but what has more value is that my children will never know what this is like. What has the most value for me is that God gets all the glory and someone gets their needs and desires fulfilled through seeing it can happen even for someone like me. It's bigger than me.

What is the value of your seed?

It is easy for someone to get stuck in the thought of the process that needs to be done to the point that they may lose sight of what comes after the process has been completed. As I am trying to find strength and willpower to complete this book and to continue on to see my next, I know that it is only in the process that it can be done. It's stretching me, beating me, and I definitely feel all of it, but I also understand that everything is working toward an end goal. I can hear about the success of others' stories all I want to, but hearing and reflecting on their success doesn't change the status of mine. Although it may hype me up for a hot second and also encourage me that I can, I can't until I do. My productivity is only as good as my own production process and this is why I cannot rely on anyone else's faith. This is personal.

This is something that has become a take-it-a-day-at-a-time type of project. If I could be real, there were plenty of times when the sight of my problems had me ready to quit praying, ready to quit believing, and ultimately ready to surrender my opportunity to see what my faith could produce. And this was after making my commitment to trust God! So I cannot be the one to give you a false image and or idea of the process, but I can guarantee every second is worth it because we aren't alone.

I've been learning something so intimate, and that is being able to encourage myself especially in the sureness of God. Every day I have to remind myself to keep going. Each day I have to give myself some grace but still not drop the ball. Each day I have to remember that even if I can't yet see it, I still have to see it. This means each day I have to push back how I feel no matter what and simply rely on what I know about the God who can bring me through!

> "If you quit on the process, You are quitting on the results"
>
> -Idowu Koyenikan

I like to look at doctors, lawyers, teachers, pilots, and all these other positions we could aspire to be. I then examine the time frame it took for those in these positions to get there. A doctor or a physician may undergo schooling for six or more years. A lawyer may invest seven plus years in their education. A pilot may dedicate three to four years. Regardless of the position, if they hadn't put in the work for the degree, they would have never received the opportunity to work in the field. Each field has its own measure of value, so it has its own measure of work. It doesn't solely take the positions having value, but someone understanding the value of what was and pursuing it.

> "For as the body without the spirit is dead, so faith without works is dead also."
>
> -James 2:26 KJV

I'm sure that, for most people in different fields, there were days they wanted to quit. I'm sure there were many opportunities for them to quit, but they endured. Their endurance involved taking the resources they had, using those resources until they obtained the ones they were hoping for. They took the time not only to look at the new position but to be prepared to work in the new position. They conditioned themselves to be sustained, knowledgeable, and teachable.

One of the most commonly quoted scriptures is Romans 8:28. Often, the part that is taken out is "All things work together for my good." There are more significant portions to the verse, but the focus right now is its truth. Everything we encounter in our season (our process) is working for our good. Each day God wakes you up because we are called for a good purpose. Your seed of faith is called for a good purpose. You are a part of a good and perfect plan, and you are a candidate for the grace, mercy, and favor of a good and perfect God.

Although some of the things we may encounter may not look like they're working in our favor, they are. That doctor could've said, "These early morning calls and studying feel draining right now, but somehow, I had to see the good in the idea that one day they'd be assisting to save lives. Do you feel the hardship of your assignment? Do you want to see the good?

To understand our "good," not only do we have to be in position for production, but we also have to position ourselves for a change of perspective. Yes! As we continue to work to see the fruits of our labor, we have to know there are also fruits in our labor. There is actually a lot more to the process than just getting to the other side of it.

Make space for the good. Where there is debt, there is room for overflow. Where there is unsuccess, there becomes room for success. Where there is lack, there is room for abundance. Where there is warfare, there is room for victory. Where there is sickness, there is space for healing. Make room for the good.

As beautiful as fall is, it is called fall for one of the most obvious reasons. During its time of transition, while at the beginning of its process, it is picture-worthy. It later takes a turn towards an ugly phase and starts to lose parts of itself. The trees start shedding as it is preparing for the next season.

This is a requirement for all of us. As we are processed, no matter how big or small, something is usually removed to make space for what is to come. Maybe your "fall" is losing the attachments of your doubt and unbelief. Maybe it is leaving an inability to be open-minded behind. Maybe for you, it's leaving the lack of trust, confidence, and diminishing fear. It's a space to shake off the remnants of what was produced by those last sets of roots.

Take a second to acknowledge your daily routines. Where do you spend most of your time? Who do you spend the most time with? What do you spend the most on? How does it affect your everyday life? Is it benefiting you or costing more time, money, and/or freedom? Is it pushing you towards your goals, desire, or miracle?

In this season, we have to make room to set ourselves up for the success of harvest. With this, we have to keep making room to hear how God is speaking to us in the process. We have to make room to understand what and how he is teaching us in the process so that we may use it for our next and for his glory. We can't be so consumed in the process itself but begin to see how we can use each thing that is a part of it to sustain us. It is not just working towards our good but for our good. This is what we use to activate your faith. Let's put all of this to work.

Everything they went through in their process of learning helped them not to mismanage what they are walking into. Someone could be hoping for money to pay off debt or bills but don't have self-control to stay out of the dollar store. Their process of having only a dollar and no tax could be teaching them how to hold it. Whatever it looks like for you and whatever you are facing, it is on purpose for purpose.

This same concept goes for not only what we are believing for right now but all things. Every no we receive can just be stirring us in the right direction to the sustaining yes. Every locked door can be stirring us into the placement of being the one with the keys. The dirt on your name, every rainy day, every moment of dry spouts, every tear you've cried, every struggle you've faced were working not for your placement but your positioning. God is not going to place you somewhere just to say you got there, but he will position you to prosper. God knows what he is doing concerning you.

If you are like me, looking at the Israelites I was like "well God, you are able to have just freed them and just brought them straight to the promised land. Why didn't you?". As I am learning more about God, I now understand…

1. God gives us free choice.
2. God knows what we need more than we do.
3. God sets everything he does to be sustained no matter how long it takes.
4. He knows how to set up all of our situations to line up & bless each other
5. Lastly, he knows if we are ready for it or not to be sustained.

God knew his people were not ready to walk in the promised land because they still didn't fully believe. Exodus 13 even tells us that if they faced war, they might change their minds and return to Egypt. God was not about to set them up for failure. With their minds not ready to be victorious, their enemies had the advantage and God simply said "not on my watch". God being sovereign, all-knowing, he will not knowingly send you into your demise. As he spoke to the earth and it became, the seasons also came into alignment so that it would all be sustained. He orchestrates everything according to his divine will and timing. Fruits bear at the right time and that is the same for us. As he made our bodies to naturally repair itself in its course, he made everything else concerning us to fall in alignment too. We will be promoted, elevated, delivered, blessed, healed, whole, made new, and/or walking in that miracle at the right time.

> "I can do all things through Christ which strengtheneth me."
>
> **- Philippians 4:13 KJV**

Thinking back on it now, I realize God did not only set them up with the door to the promised land but with everything they needed to get there. From the little things, they had the ability to walk; they were fed, had men amongst them skilled to lead and solve the many problems they had. Everything they needed to prosper in the land was already amongst them. The greatest of it all, he set them up with his words. His promise. He spoke, and it was settled. He had already taken care of their needs. They just needed to receive it.

This again stresses the need for us to learn about God and his word concerning us. Matthew 5:4 or even Psalms 31:9 can be for the grieved. Psalms 18:2 for those who need deliverance. Jeremiah 17:14 and Jeremiah 30:17 for healing. These are just a few examples of how equipped he is and on how he handles our specific needs. Without even doing the most, all you have to do is go on Google and search what God says concerning what you are believing for.

In learning from mentoring moments, something I've been asking the Lord to help me with is simply minding my business. As I have found that I am an easily distracted person, I understand that when I have my focus on what is my concern, I find that I have fewer issues in completing what needs to be done. In this, I've had to come to an understanding of what is mine to be concerned with and what is left to the Lord. What is mine to be concerned with is listening for what is happening and how to do it and when it is time to do it.

In listening, my objective is to come with a yes. I can be caught up in what it looks like and how the process of getting to the next seems impossible, but that is simply not my business. It is God's business to work out the process, and mine is to follow in pursuit. If there is a goal to reach one hundred dollars and my instruction is to put five dollars away each week without touching it, how long it's going to take is not my concern, but putting that five dollars away each week is.

> "Now on his way to Jerusalem, Jesus traveled along the border between Samaria and Galilee. As he was going into a village, ten men who had leprosy met him. They stood at a distance and called out in a loud voice, "Jesus, Master, have pity on us!" When he saw them, he said, "Go, show yourselves to the priests." And as they went, they were cleansed."
>
> -Luke 17:11-14 NIV

My favorite part, as is for many others, is "as they went." They didn't see what they had asked about right away, but in faith, the men continued on. Out of faith, they chose to be obedient. They didn't know how they were going to be healed; they just knew they were going to be healed. Following God's instructions makes all the difference in the outcome.

According to Numbers 23:19, we find that God is not a man, that he should lie. God's promises are yea and Amen, and he is faithful to his word. This earth belongs to him, and so does everything and everyone in it.

> "The earth is the LORD's, and the fullness thereof; The world, and they that dwell therein. For he hath founded it upon the seas, And established it upon the floods."
>
> -Psalms 24:1-2 KJV

If God spoke it, it is fail-proof. This means we are fail-proof. This means our battles are already won. This means victory is already ours. This means better already has our name on it. Knowing this, there may be a little more room to increase our faith. We know how the story ends!

What are some things you are learning in your process, struggle, and/or waiting period?

This seasoning process for me has been a big one, but every time I look at where I am compared to where I was, I, for one, have to tell God thank you and, for two, have to say, "Wanda, just keep believing." That is what it's all about. I have to keep going. I have finally reached a point of "by any means necessary," even if that means staying up to the crack of dawn to write a book. I am now understanding that value, process, and time are what's leading to the point of doors opening for me.

For you, this could be going through that ugly grieving process, or anxiety of waiting for the answer or miracle, or blessing to come. This could be practicing being fearless in different areas of your lives. This could mean gaining patience. Whatever it looks like, I challenge you to take a look back at whatever your "it" is and its value and measure what you are willing to do for it?

CHAPTER 4

GREEN HOUSE

Just as gardeners and farmers are concerned with the weather and seasoning of their fields, they also have to be aware of the environment for that to happen properly. If the seed isn't growing or at some point producing, there is a chance the plant isn't getting what it needs. The most common problem is that it isn't in an environment conducive to its growing process. There are, whether often or not, times where an environment that once was good for producing is no longer good. This could be it not getting enough sunlight, rain, or protection it may need because of where it's placed. Just like a plant, we too could find ourselves hitting roadblocks for growth due to our environment.

Are you seeing any areas of growth in your mindset, posture, or position in waiting, and have you been pushed further than the starting point?

Again, in Exodus, we can read about the harsh conditions the Israelites went through in Egypt and even their journey in the wilderness. We hear about the new place that they are preparing to go to. With both of those things, we also hear about how God was with them in it all. Despite all of the things God had done to prove to the Israelites that he is able and willing to deliver them, they continued to choose comfort, complacency, and complaints. Complaints when things didn't look like what they were promised. Complaints when any type of pushback came up. Complaints when they felt as though God wasn't near. Complaints when there was a little more than they had intended this "walk" to be. As I am to believe that what took so long was God preparing them for the promise, I also believe it was their personal barriers that had prolonged the process. Their unwillingness to be uprooted. They took a leap of faith to leave Egypt but seemed to have left their faith where it started.

Maybe the question isn't about the struggle to start but the struggle in keeping the commitment once in. Have you ever made a commitment to something or someone and it was more than you bargained for? Maybe it was a subscription that started with one fee and then took it upon itself to increase the price or split payments for different households. Maybe someone introduced themselves to you one way and when they got comfortable you saw a side you weren't expecting. Maybe it's something that was supposed to be quick and easy and ended up taking more time and energy than it was supposed to.

What is the first thing that comes to your mind and what was your response to it?

The Israelites knew how the story ended for them: Prosperity, property, power, and new positioning but that wasn't enough. Knowing wasn't enough for them and sometimes realistically isn't enough for some of us even if it should be. Freedom and gain are given to a mind willing to receive it. Is your mind and heart ready to receive what it is you are believing for?

On this journey of planting a seed of faith, I realized that no one made the disclaimer of how many unwarranted things would pop up during my journey or even how many times I would have to recommit myself in this process. It's widely talked about, the beauty of the process and about that initial yes but often failed to mention the yes's between the first yes and success. We don't talk about how many falls and the struggle to get back up, having to push through every day, saying yes to believing and then having to say yes to waiting on what you believe. They don't talk about the multiple changes that have to occur while waiting on change to occur or even how made up your mind really has to be.

The Israelites, just like myself at times, found themselves double-minded. Seesawing back and forth from faith to fear. This is one of those processes God has been working off of me. As I have seen such an improvement in myself, I still have a lot of work to do. I've noticed that in some areas I am dragging when this is the time to be sprinting. Where I find myself double-minded is where I know how to check my belief. This is why a made-up mind is so important. It is the difference between getting somewhere in the process and to the end of a process. Talking about making up the mind is easy. Doing it is another story. As important as it is to have a made-up mind, it is equally if not more important to understand what influences your mind. What influences your thoughts shows up in your decision-making abilities. This is why just removing them from Egypt wasn't enough. There wasn't just a need for replacement but renewing of the minds. The new placement before the "New" placement was for renewing.

> "Do not conform to the pattern of this world, but be transformed by the renewing of your mind."
>
> -Romans 12:2 NIV

Before I got to this point in my life, ready for change, I had mini battles that had to be conquered before I could face this big one. On and off in church, I've heard a lot of testimonies about how many could've, should've, and would've lost their minds. I have always been encouraged by how God kept people from literally losing their good senses. When I listen to them, I honestly can't help but reflect back on when I actually did lose my mind.

As someone who grew up in church and had a deep love for it (I didn't really have a relationship with God at this point), I found myself in a space where I said I'd never get to. In this timeframe, I was in a place where I felt like I'd been dropped. I was dealing with the results of someone else's issues and had no control over much. Going into another house, not sure what I was going to do or how I could fix what was broken, I started setting goals. I had notebooks full of goals but had no plans or willpower to reach them. Oddly enough, things started to look up.

I found a job I thoroughly enjoyed and started moving up. At first, I kept to myself and left it at that. Eventually, when starting to associate more and getting acclimated with the people and things around me, I started to break out of my shell a little and broaden my character. Just as quickly as that escalated, it wasn't too long after that I had come out of character. It happens just that fast.

Work required me to miss a few Sundays, so I became more comfortable not going when I didn't feel like it. The people that I started getting close to around me seemed to be living their best lives, and with the reality of everything around me, I thought, "It wouldn't kill me to have a little fun too". I then found myself eventually reintroducing a language I let go of, partying leading to drinking, and finally leading to smoking. As common as this is, it was completely opposite of who I am and even was at the time. I personally wasn't strong enough to handle the fire that I was in. I was also oblivious to spirits and how they transfer.

I had lost all sight of conviction. I heard the voices of others encouraging me to keep going in the habits I gained rather than God telling me to come back home. Laziness started to kick in, desires to block out everything around me all the time increased, and a mental sickness settled in that I was completely unaware of. I no longer cared about anything, anyone, or myself. I didn't even have a desire to want help or to get better. At this point, I was no longer the same. Deep down in my heart, I knew someone was still praying for little old me.

It wasn't until I started coming back to church, changing my frequent environment, that I realized how deep in it I was (I didn't come back initially in my own doing). Embarrassed, I wanted to hide the things I was doing but wasn't in a headspace to give it up. I was just lying, literally about any and everything; for absolutely no reason. I didn't want to be a liar, and I really struggled with understanding why I kept lying without hesitation. My eyes started opening to the people that I hung out with.

I like to think about the children's song that goes something like, "Be careful little eyes what you see, ears what you hear, mouth what you say, and hands what you do." All of it is an open door to your mind. We have to be watchful of the things we watch daily, the things we listen to, the things we are comfortable saying and doing, and the people who we are with. Those around you could possibly have too much access to you and too much authority over what you do and who you are. It's not safe out here in these streets.

I spent most of my time with people who smoked, drank, cheated, and lied, and I started becoming a product of my environment. I was conforming. Ice in a warm drink. While the ice is initially changing the condition of the drink when left in the wrong environment for too long, the drink starts to change the temperature of the ice. It's me, I was the ice; Melting. In this timeframe of my life, I was a walking thermometer reflecting the temperature of my environment, rather than being a thermostat setting it.

One thing about it, I had not one person to blame for where I had gotten but myself. Although what was around me influenced my thoughts, it was me personally not watching my surroundings and making the decisions. I said yes. My decision, the one thing I was able to have control over, was mishandled and I lost control and my mind in the midst of it. But I wasn't alone in the fire. With the grace of God, I wasn't strung out on drugs or an alcoholic or even someone who could only see myself in the light of club doors on the weekend, but I was someone who needed to get their mind right. I am so grateful I was able to call on God who is a mind regulator and my mind be regulated.

Between the forty years of the Israelites and my seven, there were too many mental attachments that had to be let go of in the process. Like when we have too many files and lose storage, we have to delete the attachments. For us, this attachment is not just mindsets but total mentalities; Not just what is current but the status of our everyday thinking and beliefs.

I had a self-reflection moment, and I didn't like who I had seen. It was annoying because the same people I was hanging with seemed to have no real life issues to deal with except what they created, but my reality was when I was sober my bills, debt, and the fact that I needed a home didn't just disappear. Realizing what needed to be done wasn't enough. I had to make a decision to start slowing down, which led to me stop drinking and smoking. I then had to start openly correcting myself when I lied so that I wasn't a liar. As hard as it was, each step I had to keep saying yes to God, to change, to be a better me. And I don't dot every I and don't cross every T, but my yielding made room and now I am a better me.

The field workers pay attention to detrimental things harming their fields. If a bird or animal is eating away at their produce, they set up scarecrows or wires and other things keeping the field from being harmed. If those things aren't working they step in and handle it. This is what God does for us. Not that his plans don't work but we don't always follow the plans.

Currently my favorite story in the Bible is the story of the three Hebrew boys. They already faced captivity and at the moment of their mention were up against one of the most challenging things to be faced. They along with all the others were ordered to bow to a statue that was not their God. It wasn't just a simple punishment if they didn't, It was facing the fiery furnace and being put to death. Most would say "just bow, God knows your heart". Nevertheless, these men stood their ground and said they would not bow. This was them saying yes to God all over again. This was them choosing not to conform. This was not just any yes but one of the most committed yes's. They were thrown into the furnace even with their good faith.

The outcome wasn't what was expected. A fourth man (God) was in the fire with them and they came out unharmed, not burned or even smelling like what they've been through. God didn't keep them from it but he kept them in it. I love this and can't help but think if them having each other helped to keep them committed to God. I wonder if having the right people in their corner kept reminding them who they are, whose they are, and what they believed.

For a long time, I was surrounded by people and still now I recognize some that don't mind seeing me down. I won't say they didn't "Love" me but I can say many of them had a broken idea of love. They didn't mind seeing me broken or without or falling apart because it made them feel better about themselves. I even had people take the little that I had from me knowing they had more. I've also had people give to me just so they had something to take away. NEWS FLASH (this is for me especially), it takes one time for someone to show you how they really feel about you, your time, your resources, and everything else concerning you.

What sucked was that I had to go through a period of isolation for transformation. Isolation did not mean excluding God or completely separating from people. Total separation leaves too much room to overthink and hear only your thoughts and that is not okay. That is an enemy tactic. Isolation for me meant, in some aspects I'd have to stand alone. This was a time not for agreement but alignment.

At times I felt alone! Truthfully, no matter how much closer I had gotten to God, I still found myself falling into the space of wanting to go back because it was easier. I had to let go of people I loved and a lifestyle that I was comfortable in. In this same token, I watched chains falling off of me. So I made the decision to keep walking through the fire.

Albert Einstein said it best, "Insanity is doing the same thing over and over again and expecting different results." This is what I was doing;

willing to wear unlocked chains on my mind like it was a fashion statement. I kept calling and or answering people I shouldn't have been, and revisiting ideas that did not help me grow. This was until I finally made up my mind that it was no longer for me.

Those thoughts and memories pulling us back could also be reflected in the weeds we have yet to cut. This is how some of us are now. We don't really recognize our attachments so it's hard to understand why we struggle in some areas. This could be simply struggling to look for that new job you want, struggling to apply, struggling waiting on what is coming, struggling believing what is coming, struggling to just do and or go. This is why sometimes it's possible to never really feel challenged to change at all.

Challenged! With the company we keep, there should be some challenges. Not CONTROL but CHALLENGES. There should be some level of accountability. There should be a push and or even a pull if they've gotten further than you in an area. Not everyone's concern is that they have bad company or friends but that they may not have too many people pushing them beyond where they currently are.

If you ever watch sports games (I be watching them but never know what's going on), you'd notice, let's say in track for example, the runner usually picks up speed when they hear their loved ones in the crowd cheering for them. It's always a little extra push to keep going and to give their best. Just like in the games or on the field we as humans need good supporters in our corner as well. Someone possibly annoying enough to push us into greatness. Someone to say, "how much did you put away for the car", "stop spending so much on this so you can reach your goal", "did you contact who you needed to contact", "Alright, it's time to get up. You have work to do" or even "You are good enough".

This is akin to the fieldworker; always checking on their field, watchful, ready to get dirty, hurt, or approach something that might not be good for them.

In my isolation, as I turned my ear, self, and mind away from those who maybe didn't intend to harm me but still caused collateral damage, I had to redirect my attention to those who could help fix the damage. It took a lot of letting go of my stubbornness and pride, but praise God I finally broke through. I had some sisters working with me and staying in my ear to keep me saying yes. Yes, it was my decision, but it was their belief in me that kept pushing me to be better and have more than I had.

I was very strategic in choosing whom I gave access to my ears and heart. I selected people who went through some things and came out stronger. I consulted people who weren't given everything but had to work for it. I listened to those who've been dropped and found their way back up, or failed, or lived in poverty but are now successful doing what they love. People who took a leap of faith even with uncertainty and came out okay. I had to align myself with someone who related to my process; someone who had a clue. These same people were not afraid of their stories and shared them so that someone else could rise as well. They are examples of another yes.

At this current time, two people have the biggest influences on me. One is my Bishop. My Bishop works hard and prays about EVERYTHING. I often find myself saying, "Let me pray about it first" or questioning, "Did I pray before coming up with my one solution." It's sometimes annoying because I can hear him at times I just want to do what I want to do, but still, it's for my good. The second is Evangelist Latrice Ryan. She is bold about who she is and the God she loves. She doesn't mind talking about her struggles and what led her to the point of her success. I even joined the Kingdom sniper community to be around other people trying to grow.

I listen to both of them so much that I could really do a show mimicking them down to the huffs and puffs. I know the key changes and everything. I even noticed that I sound like who I listen to in the way I talk and write now. Although that's great, in my effort to grow, I don't listen to them to be able to mimic them but to learn from them. Out of everyone I feed my thoughts with, each one of them has a different story, process, and level of success. That is going to be the same with you and me. Nothing will be identical. The common denominator in it all is that they all have faith, God, and success, and that is what we should be going for. If God can do it for them, I have no doubt that he can do it for me. It's not just about associating with their name and saying, "Those are my people," but it's actually seeing the fruit of the labor. I don't want to be one of those people who sound good and look good but are not good.

Since actively removing negative people around me and the negativity within me, I think clearly and see clearly. I am not bombarded by the thought of being okay with being stuck. I now have a desire and am making moves to better myself and change the state of who I am. Adding people with success in my ear has not only impacted me but is showing results. In just three months, a credit score I wouldn't even look at because of how bad it was has gone up over one hundred points and is still increasing. This "homeless" situation I've been dealing with for the last thirteen years, in just one year of adding positive influences, is coming to an end. And I am even now about to publish my own book. I am grateful for the people who gave me space and kept watering me with all of this dirt on me. Thank you to the people who have been praying for and with me, adding sunshine. Thank you to everyone who walked away from me.

I'm learning that while changing company, I still have to change what I am willing to receive. I can't accept new people for new levels without opening myself up for new corrections. Just as I am willing to take in the good, I have to be willing to hear and listen when someone points out potential issues. Here is the kicker: I shouldn't only hear it but examine myself and apply it. This is what the yes feels like.

This is like a diamond under pressure. Those challenging us or showing up with more than we have is an opportunity to apply pressure to the way we think, feel, react, respond, and how we go about reaching, waiting, or working for our miracle and goals. It's pure and constant motivation to keep saying yes. It's not enough to just jump into the process. Many see the process and start walking, but many don't see their way out. This is where many revolving doors show their face, and many blessings get misplaced.

Peter, a great man in the Bible between Matthew 14:22-23, took a leap of faith stepping out of the boat and walking on water with Jesus.

Quickly after he stepped out of the boat, he started paying attention to the winds and waters around him and got distracted. Peter started to sink. He took his eyes off of the one who caused him to be able to step out of the boat in the first place and lost his footing. He was human. He saw with his human eyes the dangers and detriment of what surrounded him. He had lost sight of the prize.

Y'all don't be like Peter at this moment. We have to get our minds right and focused. You have the grace to get through and stand strong. You can do this. You may not be literally walking on water, but taking a chance to go after what you want is definitely a risk in any form. It is going to be easy to see the reality of what is around you and lose faith. Winds blow hard and can shake the situation up, and we honestly have every reason to want to get back in the boat. I am challenging you to keep walking. Keep your focus. Keep your eyes on the prize. Keep your eyes on the one who gives you the ability to step out of what you are in and into better; into more. Jesus was in Peter's circle (more like Peter in Jesus' circle, but that's beside the point). Peter had someone greater than him, smarter than him, and more skilled and faith-filled teaching him. He soon became the best version of himself even while facing adversities. He has faced himself first and then faced the world. He was blessed.

I can tell you a million stories of transformations I had to encounter to get to this level of faith right now, but yours is equally important. Faith is a risk of stepping out of what you are sure of. What are some of your transformation stories? How far have you come? Use the old stories to encourage the new ones. Take some time to evaluate the areas you feel like you keep trying in. Areas where you are struggling to wait and believe. Areas where maybe you just need a little more help to keep trusting the process. After you have evaluated these things, go into deep thought about who is in your circle, taking up your time and resources. Be honest with yourself if they are pushing you into greatness, keeping you from greater, or letting you stay complacent where you are. At the same time, understand what type of person you are with others. Don't forget to be completely honest. Lastly, what are you going to do about it?

CHAPTER 5

EVERGREEN

We are at the most intentional point of this book. This Is the most impactful portion as this is where you have the ability to make a decision and go back and reflect on your thoughts through the possibilities. This is that moment of now knowing grief and hope can exist in the same exact moment. As Jesus wept over Lazarus, he grieved in human form even as he was the hope. In that exact moment hurt met hope and became whole.

As I intentionally didn't make this a step by step guide through faith I set out to give a real life current day example of realistically what faith could resemble. I told myself that this would be something I'd take to the grave but I lay my fear and pride in the casket hoping someone may not feel alone in going through life, the process, and or unbelief. I may not have much but I have plenty as I have reaped the harvest of faith. As it is common for us to hear faith building stories from the bible, I figured if we serve the God that is the same yesterday, today and forever more, the God of the bible, he surely can perform miracles, signs and wonders for us willing to receive today.

This current day generation of people have so much fighting against them and a lot of it begins in the mind. We have this complex of "nobody understands" and it's completely right. No one will ever understand how these things concerning us affect us personally but the God who sees all and knows all. He graciously gives us the ability to recognize where we are so that we can decide where we want to be. That is the grace of free choice that we have. I know we all will never experience our moments the same way no matter how similar the story line is, but the reality is all the stories can end the same; in victory and in glory.

Before we end this chapter and we make a decision of if we walk in faith or even of what we walk in faith with, I want to give the simplest passcode to having doors open for you. That one piece of the puzzle that sets precedent and ultimately influences the dynamic of every step of faith you may encounter. This is simply the TRUTH.

The truth is you have all rights to an expected end. You have all rights to a plan that is meant to prosper you and not harm you. You have all rights to being separated from any form of bondage. You know what you are going through and the truth is what goes in must come out and you have the ability to decide how you come out. As none of us really asked to be on this earth, it is with divine alignment that you are here at this time in the exact place that you need to be in.

Fa sho depending on what you believe for, it may not be the easiest situation to stay in the fire concerning, but really what do you have to lose?

I don't just believe, I know my forever home is coming and what I have to lose is all of this fear, rejection, poverty and everything else that's about to take my name out of its mouth.

We have had the opportunity to be awoken to the places where we feel like we have been left with a problem that needs problem solving. The truth is God is able to be all of those things we need. He could take us through school, work, grieving, a project, a plan, contracts, court, sentencing, toxic relationship, lost love, hurt, guilt, shame, pain, infertility, waiting, promotion, financial breakthrough, debt, instability and everything else we could possibly need to stand in faith about. We've had the opportunity to be awoken to the cost and benefits of the process. We've been awoken to the opportunities to check our environment and create a space to encourage our growth and now finally we come to a point of understanding the authority we have not only in making a decision but coming into agreement with it.

Talk is cheap but it could have a rich hold over the ear of someone who is in a moment of being weak. As trifling as the story of Eve and the snake is, it is so relatable. One conversation, led to one moment of decision making, led to one decision being made and in her case it was a fall. A plot of the enemy to get in her head. A plan to steal, kill and destroy.

Many of us battle with decisions that steal opportunities from us, kill hopes and dreams and destroy futures. With all of the influences of social media, tv, public figures and even the comparison to those around us, it is common to see us in a downward spiral compromising and forfeiting faith. The truth is, whatever and whoever our enemy is, this is their goal for us. They don't want to see you win. The craziest part of it all is that it's not by physical touch. It is usually by self-sabotage.

When we have the thoughts of what is impossible and what can't be done we turn away. When we see our bank accounts and it's not a reflection of "rich" and don't understand we can one day work (yes, I said work) our way into abundance we turn away. When we see all the others in positions and we have those thoughts to make ourselves smaller in the room or close our mouths we essentially are turning away. This is because we don't know the truth.

With the high rise of influences, there has been a high rise of mental attacks, defeat, delay, lack of wisdom and plain old ignorance. As we are not to lean on our own understanding but trust God as he directs our path, it's baffling to see how many people have to consult with others on how they should live their lives. Wise counsel, therapy and taking in sound advice is encouraged but dependence on someone to make your call to your next when they didn't call you to your now is not.

We see people asking single people for relationship advice. We see people who are stuck in similar situations asking each other for advice. We see people asking advice on how to get around the waiting or the working portions of the process. Is it sound advice?

Who has your ear? As everyone should have accountability personal in their lives we have to know who we have and where we draw our lines. It's not always those that are in our environment and or group that we consult counsel with. Who do you talk with, what are some things you go to them about and what is the response?

I couldn't believe how many people have told me that they have consulted with mediums and psychics to see about their lives. Paying people to determine the destiny that you were not designed to disrupt. And many people start altering and mishandling information trying to create either what was spoken to them or trying to work against it. With these types of things we never know the agenda of the person making a dollar off of your story and we wonder why our spirits and minds get jacked up.

This is no different with Prophets in the church. Many, even myself at a point in my life, looked for someone to call us out of these places and issues that we are in. I personally looked for someone to prophesy a book into my life when I always had the capability within me without their words, I looked for someone to tell me I'm going to get a new home and all that jazz.

I personally got none of that because one prophets came to set order, instruct and guide into what will be and two I was looking solely for what will be to just be. For a long time because I didn't get the answers I wanted how I wanted them I walked in agreement with those things said and unsaid. I didn't know the truth, but I do now.

As we have a lot of people today trying to be prophets I come here to tell you the truth is, that is not what everyone is called to be but we do have authority to prophetically speak over our own lives and situations. Prophetic speaking is telling correctly what will happen in the future.

> "The tongue has the power of life and death, and those who love it will eat its fruit."
>
> -**Proverbs 18:21 NIV**

Our own words can make or break our moments. While God has the final say, his greatness allows us to determine what the final say might look like for us. When we have negative thoughts, our conversations change, and we sound off an alarm to our demise. Let me lead off with the example of "My anxiety." When you claim it and put a "my" on there, you give ownership, agreement, and finally authority to make you anxious. This goes for all those causal statements such as "I can't," "it's not for me," "My fear," "I hate," "I don't want to," "There is no chance," and the list goes on. What are you consenting to?

I know my words are "not me," "I can't," "I'm scared" as I tend to reject myself before I allow others to. This is how I have been stopping my progression. I say them unconsciously and frequently. So, this is why I consistently have been walking in fear and inviting rejection. I even find myself speaking these things even in an intent to address them but am not always careful of how I let it come out of my mouth. Sometimes, others say things that reach my mind, and I start to believe.

What are some of your sayings? What things have you been speaking unconsciously or even consciously that may need to change? What are others speaking over you?

The truth is, these sayings can be harmful but can be reversed and can reverse your thinking. Renouncing! Renouncing is where we have the ability to fight back and cancel those things said. Our God is a forgiving God; we can simply repent for agreeing, speaking, and living out the fruits of these sayings and turn away from them. "I am not sick." "Anxiety, you have to leave." "I have a sound mind." "I no longer walk in fear." And we can say these things because they are aligned with truth.

The truth of God's words tells us fear is not for us. The truth of God's words says we are already healed by his stripes. The truth of God's word says we have a sound mind. We walk and work in the truth of his word, and there we prophesy to ourselves. His word tells me he is a provider, so I come into agreement with him as my provider, and my statement becomes "I will lack nothing." It is that easy.

Now according to your possible seed, I challenge you to speak to it. Speak truth to it. Speak life to it as a natural planter does so do we. Water your plant with your words and fuel your mind to believe.

Before you make your final decision, I want to leave the final cards of the faith of the Israelites in their path to the promised land. When the time had come, they had reached the point of preparing to fully walk into what belonged to them. After all of that waiting, working, deconstructing, reconstructing, reevaluating, and walking in faith, they were about to see what all of it was for. Twelve men went to spy on the land and bring a report back of their capabilities to obtain the land. The report they brought back didn't sound like the promise of the Lord.

> "And there we saw giants, the sons of Anak, which come of giants: and we were in our own sight as grasshoppers, and so we were in their sight."
>
> -Numbers 13:33 KJV

Fear of what they had seen talked them out of believing the God who promised it. Fear had them believing they were small and so they were. Faith isn't sight; it's belief. It didn't only talk them out of believing but it talked them out of receiving. This was so bad that they were even willing to go back to the place they had been delivered from. Contrary to those who agreed to the report and believed it, there were two who believed otherwise. Joshua and Caleb had great faith in God and in their ability to conquer the land and live in the fullness of their promise despite what it looked like. They believed and they received. This is what your decision can boil down to. You have so much power and authority. Use it.

> "Because you're not yet taking God seriously," said Jesus. "The simple truth is that if you had a mere kernel of faith, a poppy seed, say, you would tell this mountain, 'Move!' and it would move. There is nothing you wouldn't be able to tackle."
>
> -Matthew 17:20 MSG

Do you believe it?

CHAPTER 6

IN THE HOUSE

A small plastic cup inside of a home, when filled with soil, seed, and water, leaves room to house a plant. That one plant is enough to start a garden. So, a small person stepping outside of themselves to plant a seed of faith is more than enough to build a bouquet of benefits from belief.

I have had a thousand and one excuses why I couldn't get to this point that I am at right now. I had a thousand excuses why I couldn't start not my road to recovery but my road to renewal. I saw my challenges larger than my chances of success. And for a long time, I have seen my problems bigger than my problem solver. I finally took off my glasses and corrected my blurry vision. Even though I am still walking through the fog of this faith walk, I see clearer than ever. This time I will not be an example of what not to do but an example of what my faith can do.

Throughout this whole book, we experience the rollercoaster of the Israelites' path to freedom, the rollercoaster of my journey to a new life, and the rollercoaster of your journey in whatever it is you are believing for. We understand bondage in any form is not our portion and that faith is a key made to open doors. The ultimate thing we learn is that a decision has to be made. One decision that can change your moment, desire, or need. One decision that can change your life. One decision that can change your outlook and can ultimately change your outcome.

It is common that we overthink and overcomplicate the simple things. But today we acknowledge we no longer have to. As we are not putting our faith in the things of our desires, we put our faith in the God above our desires. God wants you to walk into more. He wants to bless you according to his will. He wants you to be prosperous. He wants you to be healed, whole, and made new. He wants you to walk in every open door that has your name on it. He wants you to have access to every blessing attached to you. He also wants you to want it. Your choice.

I've spent the majority of my quarter of a century on this earth filled with what I couldn't have. I was drowning in what I couldn't be. I was consumed by what I am dealing with and plagued by the thoughts of whose fault it was. I was so blinded by what I could see.*Read that again*

BUT GOD!

God took me as I was. He took me with all of my mistakes and disobedience! He took me blind, senseless, conformed, stubborn, and stuck in cycles of unbelief. Then he also took my situation that I felt like I'd never see the end of. He placed both of us in his hands and started doing a new thing. He rearranged my thinking, my stamina, my finances, my future, my hope, my faith, and now I not only believe in the impossible but I am seeing the fruits of every seed of faith that I've planted. He is ready, willing, and able to do it all for you, however it may look like on your end.

I didn't have to reach a certain measure of status. I didn't have to get into a certain financial bracket. I didn't have to be free from all of my emotions. I didn't have to be free from everything I was facing. I didn't have everything all figured out and planned. I didn't have to go looking for someone to depend on to see my way through. I didn't have to really do anything but let go of worry and grab onto faith. All I had to do was seek his face, and he stretched out his unchanging hand. All I had to do was choose to believe beyond what I could naturally see.

You don't need a special alarm to tell you it's go time. This is your alarm right here. Go for it. Pursue after what you want if it is for your good. The ground is ready to be dug to bury the seed and no longer your hope. It's time to wake up and smell the roses instead of being covered by them. Too many times you let the opportunity slip from your hand. Too many times your blessing passed you by. Now it's time to open and receive.

You don't need a special word of approval from anyone to qualify you for something. God has that power and has given us a measure of power and resources to speak to those things that be not. Open your mouth and speak what you believe and watch as some mountains start to move.

It doesn't take several panic attacks to have a moment of peace, and we learn and are reminded that God has not given us a spirit of fear but of power, love, and a sound mind according to 2 Timothy 1:7 in the bible. You have peace. You have a sound mind. You have a future with an expected end.

It doesn't take a special moment or gathering to get you to the next moment. I am proof. It was in a space by myself with all of my habits surrounding me that I sat them aside and officially said yes to God for the first time. That was the first step to changing my life forever. Did I stop doing everything right away? No. God processed me how he saw fit, and I was able to eventually stand without the things I leaned on.

For some people, they made their decision and it stopped for them immediately, and for others like me, we made our decision and it started the process for the habits to be removed.

It doesn't take a special place to hear and receive. God is always speaking. It was in the middle of a storm that I gave my life to God. It was in the middle of a storm that I received a word that it was time to get up and move. It was in the middle of a storm that I was told it won't always be like this. It was in the middle of a storm on a mattress on the floor that I said I received the word and I am getting up. It was in the middle of a storm when I was in church on a Wednesday night to hear Dr. Patricia Burks testify about her Now Faith. It was in the middle of this same storm that I began writing a book. In this same storm, God opened the door for it to be written. God opened the door for it to be published for you to read. In the middle of this storm, I was blessed by the tools housed in me. God gives us the gifts and resources inside of us. In the room. Now make room for the gifts and resources. Everything we need is right here.

Everything doesn't have to be a good sight; we just have to open our eyes of faith to see our God in sight. In this moment, you have space to be so honest with yourself about yourself. This is your opportunity to look in the mirror and choose what you want. This is your opportunity to walk out of some things and into some things. This is your opportunity to see the end of some things.

> "Better is the end of a thing than its beginning…"
>
> -Ecclesiastes 7:8 ESV

This is the end of doubt. This is the end of debt. This is the end of fear. This is the end of poverty. This is the end of brokenness. This is the end of Anxiety. This is the end of sickness. This is the end of struggle. This is the end of an over-stimulated mind. This is the end of lack. This is the end of low resources. This is the end of ……………..!

THIS IS THE END!!!

I want you to take some time and space to write an honest letter to yourself. Let it be real from you. Let it be something you can check back in with and remind yourself or give yourself a wake-up call. Be real. Be You.

CHAPTER 7
HARVEST

"But the God of all grace, who hath called us unto his eternal glory by Christ Jesus, after that ye have suffered a while, make you perfect, stablish, strengthen, settle you."

-1 Peter 5:10 KJV

Dear God,

We thank you for waking us up yet another day. We thank you for the gift of your grace. God, we thank you for your presence with us in anything we could be facing. We thank you for this seed of faith. We thank you for being trustworthy and that we can trust you with our seed. We thank you for being a safe place for it to blossom, as we recognize it is better in your hands than our own.

I am so grateful that in everything you do, there is great intention. You do all things divinely. You do all things with precision. You do all things well, even down to keeping us routing and rerouting so that we may walk the path to our expected end.

God, I am grateful for the individual that took the time to consider faith. Not just any faith but faith in you. God, as their eyes are shifting off of what is and onto what can and will be, I tell you thank you. I tell you thank you, for I know you are so much so God that you will never fail them.

God, as we reflect on things that may have gone wrong in our lives, places where we felt like we've taken a fall, places that seem to have reached a dead end or a wall of impossibility, this step of faith helps us to change our perspective. This helps us to see it for what it really is, and what it really is, is something that shall be conquered.

God, today I stand in agreement and help water the seed of faith that is growing in your grace for their good and your glory. You know what is necessary for us to receive the harvest, so God, I pray for stamina, endurance, peace in patience, strength, a sound mind, hope, and overall BELIEF. Help our unbelief, God, as we are choosing to believe you. As human as we are, it is natural for us to have curiosities and concerns, but I pray that there will be no room and no vacancies for doubt, sight, and defeat to check in, in Jesus' name.

Even if we do feel anything, today we acknowledge that we can come to you with any cares that we may have, for you care for us and are available to lift any load.

God, I believe we are about to walk into a time frame of fresh miracles, for you were, are, and will forever be a miracle worker.

Today I believe with the one who needs healing. God, whatever type of sickness it may be, we hand it over to you now. You are Rapha, God our healer. You can heal the mind, body, and soul. Today it's not about what any doctor said or even we ourselves, but it's about what you say. God, you can reach into any part of the brain, mind, cerebral chords, and make them stable. Headaches, dizzy spells, sinuses, ADHD, anxiety, autism, depression, low self-esteem, suicidal thoughts, and anything else have no authority over you, God. Any pain in the body from the crown of the head to the soles of the feet has to leave when you speak. All sickness and disease and anything that may cause discomfort stand no chance against you. Whether diseased from birth, chronic illnesses, "lifelong" illnesses, diagnosed due to our decisions, or just life happening, I believe if you can conquer the grave you can conquer what could lead us to it. God, I Believe!

God, today I believe with the one who has a need that needs to be met. Today we recognize you as Jireh, God our provider. If you can provide seasons for the earth to sustain, how much more would you do for your creation of people? God, today we acknowledge that your ways are not our way and your thoughts are not our thoughts and your math is not our math. When things don't add up to us, you make it make sense. You take little and make it much. You multiply. You speak and take nothing and make it something. If it is a job, debt consolidation, fulfilling dreams, paying rent, food on the table, cars, homes, a cure, a way out of something, or an answer, God you are mighty enough to supply. God I believe!

God, today I believe with the one who needs deliverance from anything or anywhere. You are Moshia', God our deliverer; God our savior. God, you are mighty to deliver. God, from this point on we don't have to worry if we are in poverty, a poverty mindset, homelessness, grief, long suffering that is becoming too much, struggle, fear, hopelessness, restlessness, anger, pride, habits, lifestyles, connected to people, or anything that doesn't benefit us, for we willingly yield ourselves to you, who you are and your ability. Defeated, oppressed, and bound are not who we are. Any spirits, need to feel needed, places of negative control, bondage of saying yes to everyone and everything else that can take your people out, God, we ask that you sever the ties to them. And it is so as we believe. God I believe!

God, today I believe with the person who is simply in need of a miracle. I believe with the person who is believing for someone else. I believe with the person that is praying for someone else. I am believing with the one that loses focus and or has a hard time completing or seeing their way through to the end. I am believing with the one who still has a hard time fully understanding faith and anything concerning you. God I believe!

God I believe in the timeframe you have set that people will know you as Rapha as you've healed them. God I believe someone will know you as Jireh as you will provide. I believe someone will know you as a deliverer as you shall set the captive free just like you did for the Israelites and you are doing for me. God I believe someone will know you as hope. I believe someone will know you as their strength. I believe someone will know you as joy. I believe someone will know you as Shalom, their peace. I believe someone will know you as a way maker and a promise keeper. I believe someone will know you as a father and a friend. I believe someone will know you as the judge in the courtroom. I believe someone will know you as the one who saved their family member. I believe someone will know you as their restorer, their great redeemer, the author and finisher of their fate. I believe someone will move from breaking down to breaking through. I believe that someone is moving from sick to healed. I believe that someone is moving from half to whole. I'm believing someone is moving from hurt to well. I believe that someone is moving from wondering to knowing. I believe that someone will be going from making up their mind about something to managing it. I believe doors will be open and doors will be shut. I believe lives will be changed, and God, you will be glorified. God as I believe with those who are having faith in you, I am willing to mess around and find out who you will be in my life next. I believe you for me and those connected to me as well. God I believe as many of us will be tested through our faith I believe that we will also soon testify to your faithfulness. God I believe. God I believe. God I believe.

Nevertheless, I believe in your will over anything. God I understand the possibility of what we are believing for not to come in the timing we think it should, the way we think it should, where or even through how. I still stand on believing in you. You are sovereign and know best so we know whatever way you make it happen, it was for our good. It is well with me. No matter what it looks like, I am grateful that in hope I don't have to consider the possibility of my desire but In faith I can anticipate that IT WILL HAPPEN how you see fit.

I thank you for hearing and partnering with us in faith. Over all things, I thank you for the gift of your presence. It is in your presence that we find everything that we need. God, as your hand plays a major role in the things we obtain, I recognize that it is only in who you are that we are fulfilled. AMEN, -The planter

> "For I reckon that the sufferings of this present time are not worthy to be compared with the glory which shall be revealed in us."
>
> **Romans 8:18 KJV**

I couldn't share the greatness of putting our faith in God if I hadn't witnessed it for myself. I've seen the infertile give birth, the depressed find real joy again, the suicidal choose to live and save lives, and the underdog become the one everyone needs. As I reflect on these transformations, I can believe for what will be done. Though I am currently in the midst of a storm, it's not a story to tell only once I've gotten through it; this is my Now Faith! And I believe. Do you?

Take a space to write whatever is on your mind. This can be for your own prayer, curiosities, questions, disbelief. Write what feels right to you.

'S JOURNAL

The rest of this book belongs to you. Journal your experience believing, where you struggle, where you've seen fruit, when you may be weary waiting, when you don't want to want to believe any more, If you are having trouble accepting how it came about and even how it worked for your good.

Feel free to share your experience at

FightbyFaith@gmail.com! We are in this together.

....
....
....
....
....
....
....
....
....
....
....
....
....
....
....